U.S. Armed Forces

The Air Force Space Command

by Carrie A. Braulick

Reading Consultant:
Barbara J. Fox
Reading Specialist
North Carolina State University

Capstone
press.
Mankato, Minnesota

Blazers is published by Capstone Press,
151 Good Counsel Drive, P.O. Box 669, Mankato, Minnesota 56002.
www.capstonepress.com

Library of Congress Cataloging-in-Publication Data
Braulick, Carrie A., 1975–
    The Air Force Space Command/by Carrie A. Braulick.
    p. cm.—(Blazers. U.S. Armed Forces.)
    Includes bibliographical references and index.
    Summary: "Describes the Air Force Space Command, including its
members, equipment, and missions"—Provided by publisher.
    ISBN-13: 978-1-4296-0829-9 (hardcover)
    ISBN-10: 1-4296-0829-3 (hardcover)
    1. United States. Air Force Space Command—Juvenile literature. 2.
Astronautics, Military—United States—Juvenile literature. I. Title. II. Series.
UG1523.B73 2007
358'.80973—dc22   2007013619

Editorial Credits
Mandy Robbins, editor; Juliette Peters, set designer; Jason Knudson and
    Kyle Grenz, book designers; Jo Miller, photo researcher

Photo Credits
DVIC, 12, 13, 20–21; A1C Heather M. Forrest, 17; SRA Jacqueline Kabuyen,
    4–5; SRA Jeremy S. Smith, 8–9; SRA Pam Taubman, 28–29;
    Staff Sgt. Gary R.Coppage, 25; TSGT James Pearson, 16 (top);
    TSGT Richard Freeland, 24
NASA Johnson Space Center, 14–15
U.S. Air Force photo, cover (background), 16 (bottom), 19, 26, 27; Artwork
    courtesy Lockheed Martin, 10–11; Senior Master Sgt. John Rohrer, 22–23;
    SSGT Don Branum, cover (foreground);
U.S. Navy Photo by PH2 Michael B.W. Watkins, 6–7

**Capstone Press thanks the Air Force Space Command for their assistance
with this book.**

The Air Force Space Command does not officially endorse this book.

Table of Contents

Lifesaving Satellites

A U.S. military plane gets shot down. The pilot bails out. He finds himself lost in enemy land.

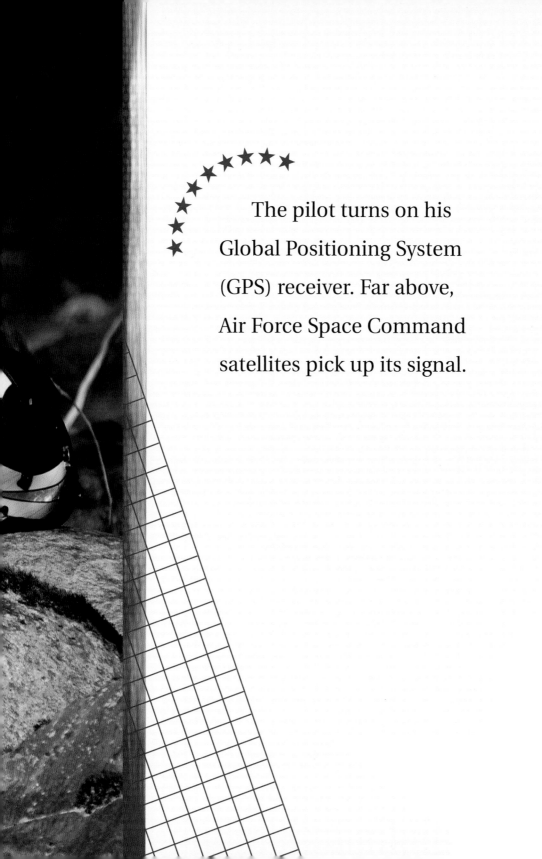

The pilot turns on his
Global Positioning System
(GPS) receiver. Far above,
Air Force Space Command
satellites pick up its signal.

The satellites show the pilot's location on the receiver's screen. The pilot uses his radio to call for help. Soon he is rescued. Space Command satellites helped save his life.

BLAZER FACT

GPS satellites can guide a weapon to a target less than 10 feet (3 meters) wide.

9

Missions

Space Command equipment is far above Earth. Space Command launches satellites that gather information as they circle Earth.

GPS satellite

★★★★★★★★★★★★★★

Minuteman III ICBM

Space Command also has the military's deadliest nuclear missiles. These weapons can travel more than 6,000 miles (9,660 kilometers).

BLAZER FACT

Space Command missiles are
called intercontinental ballistic
missiles (ICBMs) because they
can easily reach other continents.

Minuteman III ICBM

Equipment

Each Space Command satellite has an important job. Defense Support Program satellites detect missile launches from anywhere in the world.

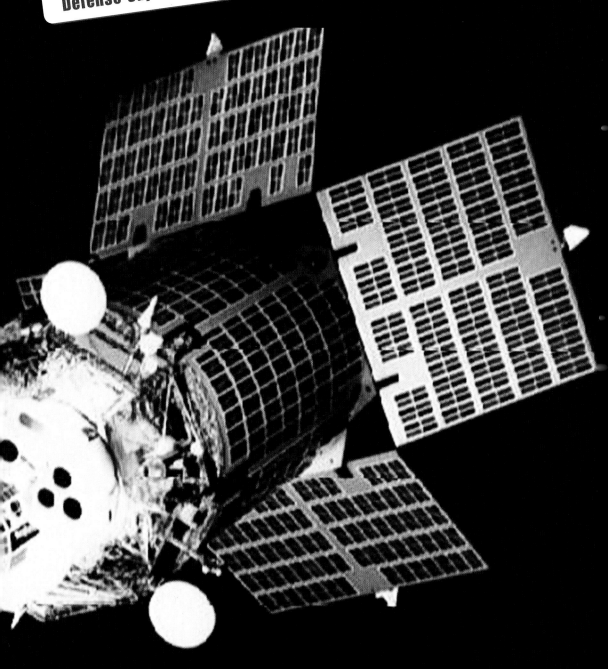

Defense Support Program satellite

★★★★★★★★★★★★★

GPS satellite dish

GPS receiver

GPS satellites can pinpoint any location on Earth. Getting lost is impossible using GPS. The military also uses GPS signals to move troops and aim weapons.

Satellites can weigh as much as 20,000 pounds (9,000 kilograms). Rockets with powerful engines blast these huge satellites into space.

Atlas V rocket

19

GPS Satellite

transmitters

solar panels

antenna

solar panels

Space Command at Work

Space Command crews
work day and night. Some
crews track satellites and other
objects in space. Other crews
launch and control satellites.

BLAZER FACT

Space Command crews keep track of more than 15,000 objects circling Earth.

Space Command crews also keep nuclear missiles ready to use. They replace old parts and fix launch equipment.

Space Command crews work
behind the scenes. You may never see
them. But they keep the country safe
and the military running smoothly.

BLAZER FACT

Space Command crews also help launch space shuttles for NASA.

Blast off!

Glossary

Global Positioning System (GLOH-buhl puh-ZI-shuh-ning SISS-tuhm)—an electronic tool used to find the location of a person or object anywhere on Earth; it is often called GPS.

intercontinental (in-tur-con-tuh-NEN-tuhl)— able to travel between continents

nuclear (NOO-klee-ur)—describes a type of power created by splitting atoms; atoms are the smallest part of a substance.

receiver (ri-SEE-vur)—a device that receives radio signals and turns them into sound or pictures

satellite (SAT-uh-lite)—a spacecraft that circles Earth; satellites gather and send information.

signal (SIG-nuhl)—information sent to or from a satellite

Read More

Cooper, Jason. *U.S. Air Force.* Vero Beach, Fla.: Rourke Pub., 2004.

Johnson, Rebecca L. *Satellites.* Cool Science. Minneapolis: Lerner, 2006.

Rosinsky, Natalie. *Satellites and the GPS.* Simply Science. Minneapolis: Compass Point Books, 2004.

Internet Sites

FactHound offers a safe, fun way to find Internet sites related to this book. All of the sites on FactHound have been researched by our staff.

Here's how:

1. Visit *www.facthound.com*
2. Choose your grade level.
3. Type in this special code **1429608293** for age-appropriate sites. You may also browse subjects by clicking on letters, or by clicking on pictures or words.
4. Click on the **Fetch It** button.

FactHound will fetch the best sites for you!

Index